Rhythm Only
Book 1

Difficulty Levels 1-5
Eighths and Sixteenths
Assorted Meters

Rhythm Only – Book 1 – Eighths and Sixteenths – Assorted Meters by Nathan Petitpas, published by Dots and Beams, Toronto, Ontario, Canada.

ISBN 978-1-9990356-4-8

www.DotsandBeams.com

Contents

About Dots and Beams

Have you ever created a musical exercise, for yourself or for a student, that would have been much more effective if you could just find a few pages of a certain type of reading material? Perhaps you're a drummer looking for pages of rhythms for developing your timing or coordination. Or maybe you're a pianist looking for melodic reading material to play in your right hand to help develop coordination with a difficult ostinato or bass line. Perhaps you're an experienced musician learning a second instrument; you may feel you would benefit from pages of random notes on a staff to help you become familiar with your new instrument. Or maybe you'd like to mix up your scale practice by playing your scales in unpredictable rhythms rather than the patterns you have been using for years. Maybe you've always played guitar by ear and have lately been wanting to learn to read music; you might want something graduated and systematic to read to help you learn the elements of musical notation but you don't want to play nursery rhymes.

Dots and Beams was created to provide a wide variety of reading materials for musicians at all skill levels and for all instruments.

My approach to creating reading material is slightly different from other approaches I've seen. Many other sight-reading books provide a series of musical compositions for use in practising sight-reading. Rather than provide books of compositions, my approach is to break down the language of musical notation into its rhythmic and melodic components and introduce these components to the user in a systematic way.

These pages of notes and rhythms are not intended to be seen as compositions: they do not follow any particular harmonic or melodic structure and the melodies they contain are not repetitive or memorable. They are exercises in which the complexity of the written language of music gradually increases in order to strengthen the user's ability to process the raw data of musical notation. While the Dots and Beams books are an excellent resource to help improve your sight-reading, their unique construction ensures that the additional uses for these books are as varied and individual as the musicians using them.

Each book in the Dots and Beams collection focuses on a specific element of musical notation. This ensures that you always have the perfect reading material for any exercise so that you can isolate the specific areas in your playing that you feel you need to work on. These books offer very little in the way of explanation and descriptions in an effort to provide as much note-reading material as possible. This is not so much a method book as it is a tool to help make practice more focused and effective.

My hope is that this collection will be one that you will revisit year after year as you find newer, more creative, and more challenging ways to use the materials to push your playing, and your students' playing, to new levels.

About the Author

Nathan Petitpas is a percussionist living in Toronto, Ontario, Canada. He works predominantly as a freelancer in the Ontario orchestral scene as well as the Toronto contemporary music scene. He teaches drum set, percussion, music theory, and general music classes in a variety of programs across Toronto. Nathan holds a Master of Music degree from the University of Toronto and a Bachelor of Music degree from Acadia University, both in percussion performance.

Preface: How To Use This Book

This collection presents the user with a series of increasingly difficult rhythms on a single pitch.

The rhythmic material in this series is organized into 10 difficulty levels. Each difficulty level contains four exercises in each of the following time signatures: 2/4, 3/4, 4/4, 6/8, 9/8, and 12/8. This gives exercises in 2, 3, and 4 beats per bar in both simple and compound meters. The first two exercises of each time signature have no ties while the remaining two exercises in each time signature include ties. In Book 1 of this series you'll find difficulty levels 1 to 5, while Book 2 completes the set with levels 6 to 10.

To curate the difficulty levels I looked at all of the possible ways we can use eighth-notes and sixteenth-notes to subdivide a single beat without the use of tuplets. The lowest difficulty level is comprised of the easiest of these one-beat rhythmic groupings. Subsequent difficulty levels include more challenging groupings while continuing to use the easier ones from previous chapters. In this way the difficulty levels are cumulative: level 1 uses only the easiest groupings, but by level 9, all of the possible rhythmic groupings have been introduced. Level 10 increases the density of challenging groupings by omitting the easier ones. The introductory page of each chapter introduces the rhythmic groupings that will be added or omitted in that chapter. On some occasions rhythmic groupings are respelled; however, these new spellings are not formally introduced at the beginning of the chapter.

The exercises in this collection are intentionally random and difficult to internalize. In keeping the rhythmic material as unpredictable as possible the door is left open for the materials to be used in many ways. It also forces the user to process every rhythm as its own event without relying on pattern recognition for help.

Some suggestions for how to use this book include:

- Practice sight-reading. The goal in practising sight-reading is not to learn the material but to develop the skill of reading new material. When practising sight-reading I encourage you to cycle through exercises quickly rather than mastering each one.
- Use a metronome! The most important thing you can do with this material is learn how to read these rhythms and play them in time.
- Advanced metronome work: Placing the metronome click on non-strong beats forces you to take responsibility for the time in a different way and trains you to hear how your rhythm relates to each subdivision of the beat. For example, instead of putting the metronome click on each quarter-note in 4/4, play the exercise with the metronome giving the second eighth note of each beat, or the last sixteenth note, or beats 2 and 4, or every third sixteenth note. Be creative with this one; the possibilities are limitless!
- Develop independence between hands by playing a repeating pattern in one hand while reading an exercise in the other. Expand on this by adding patterns in hands and feet while reading a rhythm with a remaining limb. This is a great exercise for drummers and percussionists but any instrumentalist could benefit from coordination practice.
- Use these rhythms to practice scales. Instead of playing scales in straight sixteenth-notes, try playing them in the rhythms given in these exercises.
- Write in sticking patterns, dynamics, accents, phrase marks, or other articulations for you or your students to practice. If you're not happy with the ties I included, feel free to add some of your own.
- Combine the above exercises in any way that you think will be beneficial to your practice.

As with any of the Dots and Beams books, the uses for this particular collection are limited only by the imagination of the musician using it. I encourage anybody using this book to find as many uses for these exercises as possible.

Chapter 1:

Difficulty Level 1

Simple Time

Introducing Rhythms:

Difficulty Level 1 - Simple Time

Exercise 1 (2/4 Time)

Difficulty Level 1 - Simple Time

Exercise 2 (2/4 Time)

Difficulty Level 1 - Simple Time

Exercise 3 (2/4 Time)

Difficulty Level 1 - Simple Time
Exercise 4 (2/4 Time)

Difficulty Level 1 - Simple Time

Exercise 5 (3/4 Time)

Difficulty Level 1 - Simple Time

Exercise 6 (3/4 Time)

Difficulty Level 1 - Simple Time

Exercise 7 (3/4 Time)

Difficulty Level 1 - Simple Time

Exercise 8 (3/4 Time)

Difficulty Level 1 - Simple Time

Exercise 9 (4/4 Time)

Difficulty Level 1 - Simple Time
Exercise 10 (4/4 Time)

www.DotsandBeams.com

Difficulty Level 1 - Simple Time

Exercise 11 (4/4 Time)

Difficulty Level 1 - Simple Time
Exercise 12 (4/4 Time)

Chapter 2:

Difficulty Level 1
Compound Time

Introducing Rhythms:

Difficulty Level 1 - Compound Time
Exercise 1 (6/8 Time)

Difficulty Level 1 - Compound Time

Exercise 2 (6/8 Time)

Difficulty Level 1 - Compound Time

Exercise 3 (6/8 Time)

Difficulty Level 1 - Compound Time

Exercise 4 (6/8 Time)

Difficulty Level 1 - Compound Time
Exercise 5 (9/8 Time)

Difficulty Level 1 - Compound Time

Exercise 6 (9/8 Time)

Difficulty Level 1 - Compound Time

Exercise 7 (9/8 Time)

www.DotsandBeams.com

Difficulty Level 1 - Compound Time

Exercise 8 (9/8 Time)

Difficulty Level 1 - Compound Time

Exercise 9 (12/8 Time)

Difficulty Level 1 - Compound Time

Exercise 10 (12/8 Time)

www.DotsandBeams.com

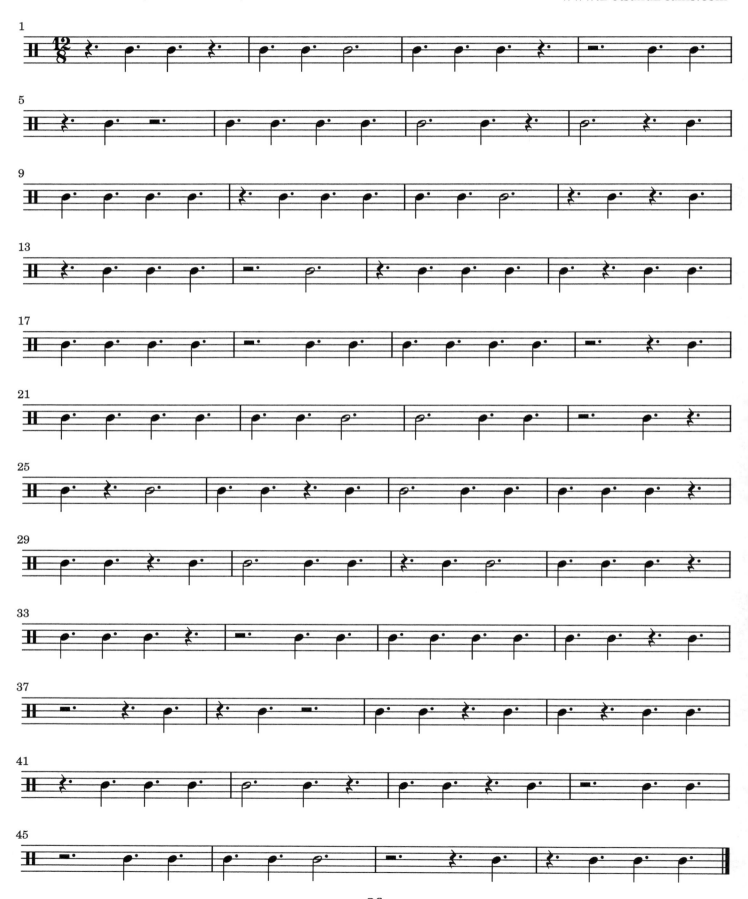

Difficulty Level 1 - Compound Time

Exercise 11 (12/8 Time)

Difficulty Level 1 - Compound Time

Exercise 12 (12/8 Time)

www.DotsandBeams.com

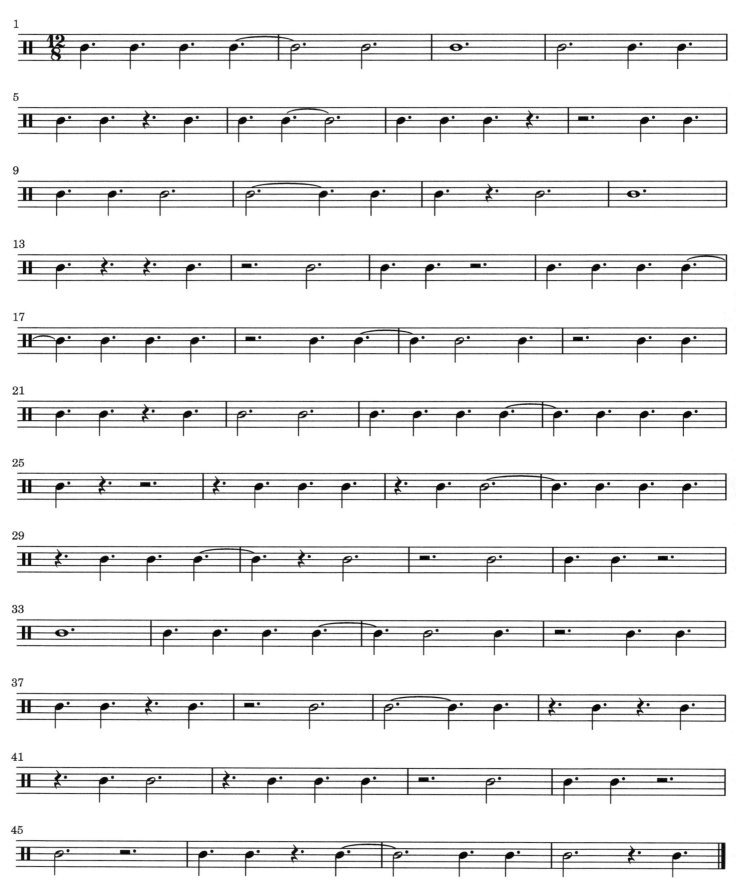

Chapter 3:

Difficulty Level 2
Simple Time

Introducing Rhythm:

Difficulty Level 2 - Simple Time
Exercise 1 (2/4 Time)

Difficulty Level 2 - Simple Time

Exercise 2 (2/4 Time)

Difficulty Level 2 - Simple Time

Exercise 3 (2/4 Time)

www.DotsandBeams.com

32

Difficulty Level 2 - Simple Time
Exercise 4 (2/4 Time)

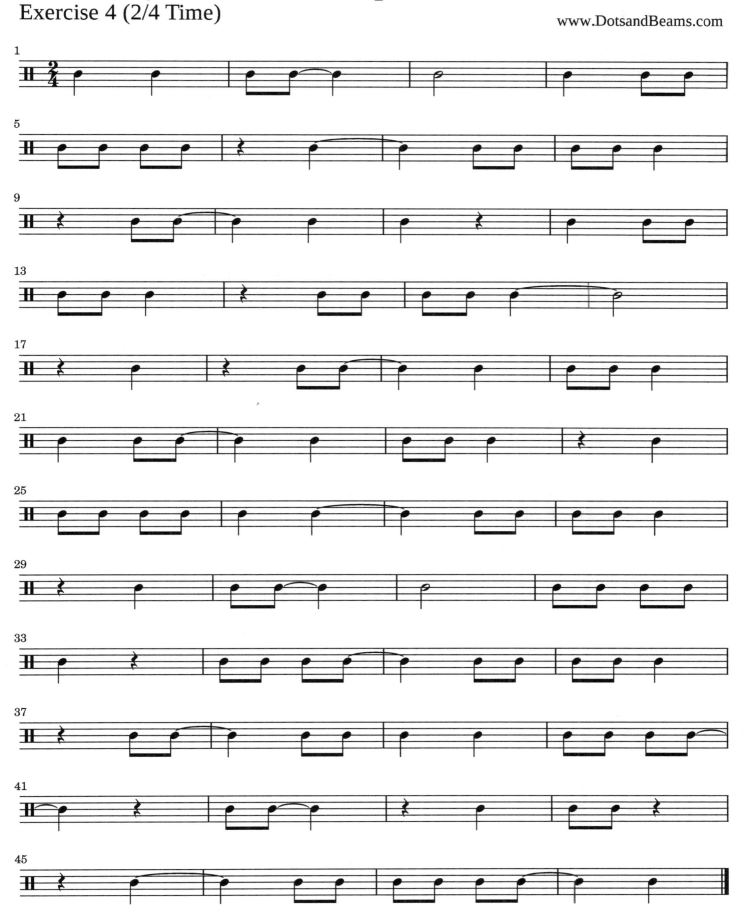

Difficulty Level 2 - Simple Time

Exercise 5 (3/4 Time)

Difficulty Level 2 - Simple Time

Exercise 6 (3/4 Time)

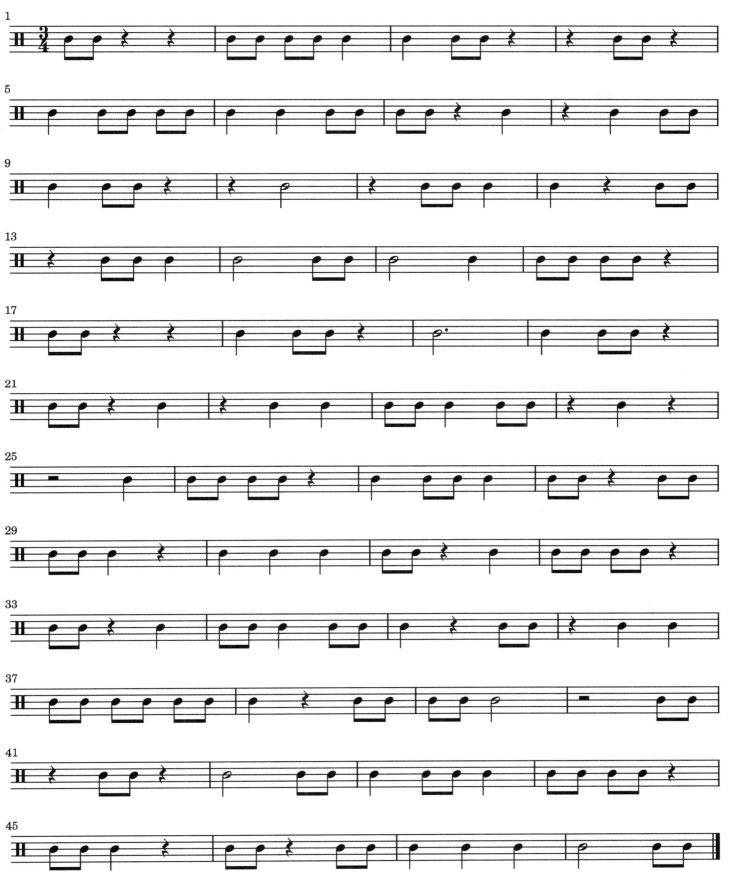

Difficulty Level 2 - Simple Time

Exercise 7 (3/4 Time)

Difficulty Level 2 - Simple Time

Exercise 8 (3/4 Time)

Difficulty Level 2 - Simple Time

Exercise 9 (4/4 Time)

www.DotsandBeams.com

Difficulty Level 2 - Simple Time

Exercise 10 (4/4 Time)

39

Difficulty Level 2 - Simple Time

Exercise 11 (4/4 Time)

Difficulty Level 2 - Simple Time

Exercise 12 (4/4 Time)

www.DotsandBeams.com

Chapter 4:

Difficulty Level 2

Compound Time

Introducing Rhythm:

Difficulty Level 2 - Compound Time
Exercise 1 (6/8 Time)

Difficulty Level 2 - Compound Time

Exercise 2 (6/8 Time)

www.DotsandBeams.com

44

Difficulty Level 2 - Compound Time
Exercise 3 (6/8 Time)

Difficulty Level 2 - Compound Time

Exercise 4 (6/8 Time)

Difficulty Level 2 - Compound Time

Exercise 5 (9/8 Time)

www.DotsandBeams.com

Difficulty Level 2 - Compound Time
Exercise 6 (9/8 Time)

Difficulty Level 2 - Compound Time
Exercise 7 (9/8 Time)

Difficulty Level 2 - Compound Time

Exercise 8 (9/8 Time)

Difficulty Level 2 - Compound Time
Exercise 9 (12/8 Time)

Difficulty Level 2 - Compound Time

Exercise 10 (12/8 Time)

Difficulty Level 2 - Compound Time

Exercise 11 (12/8 Time)

www.DotsandBeams.com

Difficulty Level 2 - Compound Time
Exercise 12 (12/8 Time)

Chapter 5:

Difficulty Level 3
Simple Time

Introducing Rhythm:

Difficulty Level 3 - Simple Time

Exercise 1 (2/4 Time)

Difficulty Level 3 - Simple Time

Exercise 2 (2/4 Time)

Difficulty Level 3 - Simple Time
Exercise 3 (2/4 Time)

Difficulty Level 3 - Simple Time
Exercise 4 (2/4 Time)

Difficulty Level 3 - Simple Time
Exercise 5 (3/4 Time)

Difficulty Level 3 - Simple Time
Exercise 6 (3/4 Time)

www.DotsandBeams.com

Difficulty Level 3 - Simple Time

Exercise 7 (3/4 Time)

Difficulty Level 3 - Simple Time
Exercise 8 (3/4 Time)

Difficulty Level 3 - Simple Time

Exercise 9 (4/4 Time)

64

Difficulty Level 3 - Simple Time

Exercise 10 (4/4 Time)

Difficulty Level 3 - Simple Time
Exercise 11 (4/4 Time)

Difficulty Level 3 - Simple Time

Exercise 12 (4/4 Time)

Chapter 6:

Difficulty Level 3

Compound Time

Introducing Rhythms:

Difficulty Level 3 - Compound Time
Exercise 1 (6/8 Time)

Difficulty Level 3 - Compound Time

Exercise 2 (6/8 Time)

Difficulty Level 3 - Compound Time

Exercise 3 (6/8 Time)

www.DotsandBeams.com

Exercise 4 (6/8 Time)

Difficulty Level 3 - Compound Time

Exercise 5 (9/8 Time)

Difficulty Level 3 - Compound Time

Exercise 6 (9/8 Time)

Difficulty Level 3 - Compound Time

Exercise 7 (9/8 Time)

www.DotsandBeams.com

Difficulty Level 3 - Compound Time

Exercise 8 (9/8 Time)

Difficulty Level 3 - Compound Time

Exercise 9 (12/8 Time)

Difficulty Level 3 - Compound Time
Exercise 10 (12/8 Time)

Difficulty Level 3 - Compound Time

Exercise 11 (12/8 Time)

Difficulty Level 3 - Compound Time
Exercise 12 (12/8 Time)

Chapter 7:

Difficulty Level 4

Simple Time

Introducing Rhythm:

Difficulty Level 4 - Simple Time

Exercise 1 (2/4 Time)

Difficulty Level 4 - Simple Time

Exercise 2 (2/4 Time)

Difficulty Level 4 - Simple Time

Exercise 3 (2/4 Time)

Difficulty Level 4 - Simple Time

Exercise 4 (2/4 Time)

Difficulty Level 4 - Simple Time

Exercise 5 (3/4 Time)

Difficulty Level 4 - Simple Time
Exercise 6 (3/4 Time)

Difficulty Level 4 - Simple Time

Exercise 7 (3/4 Time)

Difficulty Level 4 - Simple Time
Exercise 8 (3/4 Time)

Difficulty Level 4 - Simple Time

Exercise 9 (4/4 Time)

Difficulty Level 4 - Simple Time
Exercise 10 (4/4 Time)

Difficulty Level 4 - Simple Time

Exercise 11 (4/4 Time)

Difficulty Level 4 - Simple Time
Exercise 12 (4/4 Time)

Chapter 8:

Difficulty Level 4

Compound Time

Introducing Rhythms:

Difficulty Level 4 - Compound Time

Exercise 1 (6/8 Time)

Difficulty Level 4 - Compound Time

Exercise 2 (6/8 Time)

www.DotsandBeams.com

Difficulty Level 4 - Compound Time
Exercise 3 (6/8 Time)

Difficulty Level 4 - Compound Time

Exercise 4 (6/8 Time)

www.DotsandBeams.com

Difficulty Level 4 - Compound Time
Exercise 5 (9/8 Time)

Difficulty Level 4 - Compound Time

Exercise 6 (9/8 Time)

Difficulty Level 4 - Compound Time

Exercise 7 (9/8 Time)

Difficulty Level 4 - Compound Time

Exercise 8 (9/8 Time)

Difficulty Level 4 - Compound Time

Exercise 9 (12/8 Time)

Difficulty Level 4 - Compound Time

Exercise 10 (12/8 Time)

Difficulty Level 4 - Compound Time

Exercise 11 (12/8 Time)

www.DotsandBeams.com

Difficulty Level 4 - Compound Time

Exercise 12 (12/8 Time)

Chapter 9:

Difficulty Level 5
Simple Time

Introducing Rhythms:

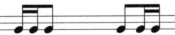

Difficulty Level 5 - Simple Time

Exercise 1 (2/4 Time)

Difficulty Level 5 - Simple Time

Exercise 2 (2/4 Time)

Difficulty Level 5 - Simple Time

Exercise 3 (2/4 Time)

Difficulty Level 5 - Simple Time

Exercise 4 (2/4 Time)

Difficulty Level 5 - Simple Time

Exercise 5 (3/4 Time)

Difficulty Level 5 - Simple Time
Exercise 6 (3/4 Time)

Difficulty Level 5 - Simple Time

Exercise 7 (3/4 Time)

Difficulty Level 5 - Simple Time

Exercise 8 (3/4 Time)

Difficulty Level 5 - Simple Time
Exercise 9 (4/4 Time)

Difficulty Level 5 - Simple Time

Exercise 10 (4/4 Time)

Difficulty Level 5 - Simple Time

Exercise 11 (4/4 Time)

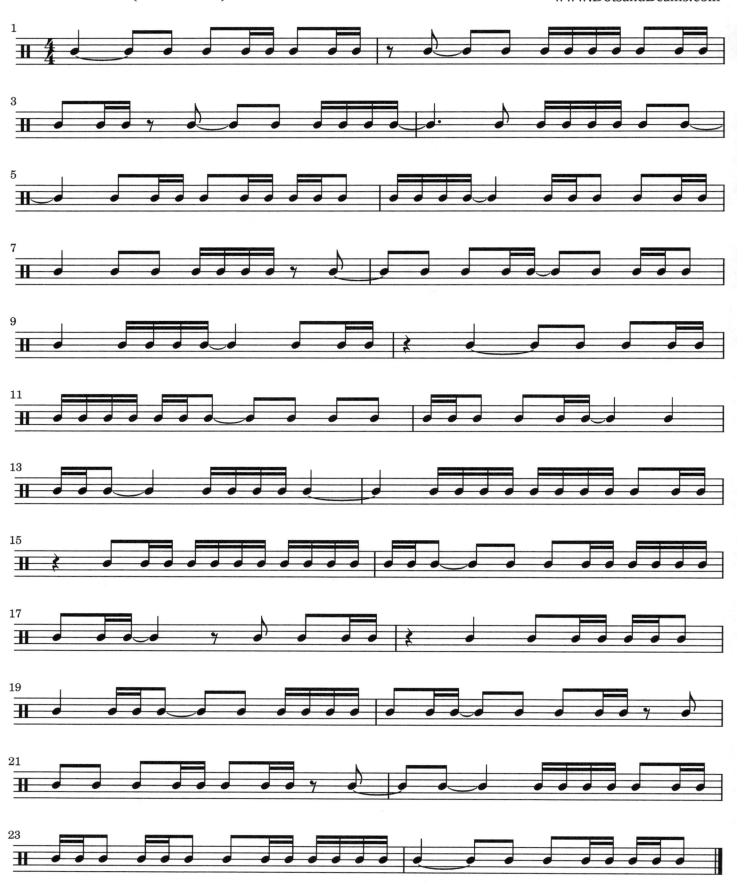

Difficulty Level 5 - Simple Time

Exercise 12 (4/4 Time)

119

Chapter 10:

Difficulty Level 5

Compound Time

Introducing Rhythms:

Difficulty Level 5 - Compound Time

Exercise 1 (6/8 Time)

Difficulty Level 5 - Compound Time

Exercise 2 (6/8 Time)

www.DotsandBeams.com

Difficulty Level 5 - Compound Time

Exercise 3 (6/8 Time)

Difficulty Level 5 - Compound Time

Exercise 4 (6/8 Time)

Difficulty Level 5 - Compound Time

Exercise 5 (9/8 Time)

www.DotsandBeams.com

Difficulty Level 5 - Compound Time
Exercise 6 (9/8 Time)

Difficulty Level 5 - Compound Time

Exercise 7 (9/8 Time)

Difficulty Level 5 - Compound Time
Exercise 8 (9/8 Time)

www.DotsandBeams.com

Difficulty Level 5 - Compound Time

Exercise 9 (12/8 Time)

Difficulty Level 5 - Compound Time
Exercise 10 (12/8 Time)

Difficulty Level 5 - Compound Time

Exercise 11 (12/8 Time)

Difficulty Level 5 - Compound Time

Exercise 12 (12/8 Time)

Thank You!

For more materials please visit
www.DotsandBeams.com

CPSIA information can be obtained
at www.ICGtesting.com
Printed in the USA
LVHW060609111019
633869LV00004B/13/P